Design: Jill Coote
Recipe Photography: Peter Barry
Recipe Styling: Jacqueline Bellefontaine,
Helen Burdett, Bridgeen Deery and
Wendy Devenish
Jacket and Illustration Artwork: Jane Winton,
courtesy Bernard Thornton Artists, London
Editor: Laura Potts

CLB 3353
© 1993 CLB Publishing, Godalming, Surrey, England
All rights reserved
This edition published in Australia in 1993 by
THE BOOK COMPANY INTERNATIONAL PTY LTD.,
9/9 WINBOURNE ROAD, BROOKVALE 2100,
SYDNEY, NSW, AUSTRALIA
Printed and bound in Singapore
ISBN 1-85833-128-5

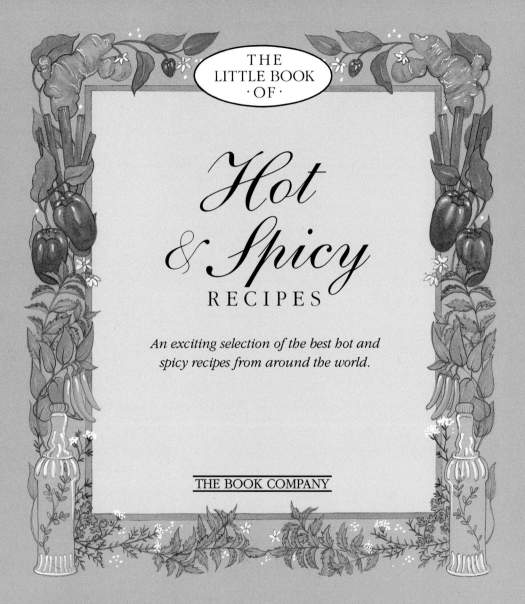

THE
LITTLE BOOK
· OF ·

Hot
& Spicy
RECIPES

*An exciting selection of the best hot and
spicy recipes from around the world.*

THE BOOK COMPANY

Introduction

Spices – the dried seeds, pods, berries, roots, stems, or buds of aromatic plants – play a vital part in the culinary traditions of many nations. In the past, spices were vital both for preserving and flavouring food, and as such were a very valuable commodity. As methods of food preservation have become more sophisticated, however, the value of spices has dropped. This, coupled with the fact that spices are more widely grown and can be more cheaply transported, has seen an increase in the variety of spices which are available and their use in everyday cookery.

A wide selection of pre-ground spices is available in most supermarkets, and are frequently the preferred choice. It is advisable, however, when buying pre-ground spices not to buy too large a quantity, as they lose much of their aroma and flavour if they are stored over a long period of time. This loss of pungency can be avoided, to a degree, by ensuring that the spices are kept out of direct sunlight, either by storing them in tinted glass jars or in a cupboard. Though more time-consuming, grinding spices, as and when you need them, is the best way to get the strongest, truest flavour.

Grinding spices can be done either by hand with a pestle and mortar, or in a small coffee grinder, kept specifically for the purpose.

Spices are usually associated with the cuisines of countries where the climate is very hot. This is not simply because this is the climate in which the plants flourish. Spices are still used widely as a preservative, lengthening the time which foods can be kept, an important function in hot countries, where vegetables and meats go off rapidly. They also help to stimulate appetites which are flagging in the heat. Fresh or dried chilli peppers and cayenne pepper, for example, will add fire to any dish. Yet, food can be spicy without being very hot. Spices such as cumin, coriander and cinnamon can lend flavour and fragrance to a dish, without being overpoweringly hot.

The recipes in this book come from around the world, and include favourites from Indian, Mexican and Chinese cuisine. They show the different ways in which herbs and spices are used, and the diversity of delicious flavours that can be achieved with even the simplest mixture of spices.

Hot and Sour Seafood Soup

SERVES 4

This interesting combination of flavours and ingredients makes a sophisticated beginning to an informal meal.

PREPARATION: 20 mins
COOKING: 20 mins

3 dried Chinese mushrooms
1 tbsp vegetable oil
120g/4oz prawns, shelled and deveined
1 red chilli, seeded and finely sliced
1 green chilli, seeded and finely sliced
½ tsp lemon rind, cut into thin slivers
2 spring onions, sliced
560ml/1 pint fish stock
1 tbsp Worcestershire sauce
1 tbsp light soy sauce
60g/2oz whitefish fillets
1 cake of fresh bean curd, diced
1 tbsp lemon juice
1 tsp sesame seeds
1 tsp fresh coriander, finely chopped (optional)

Step 1 Soak the dried Chinese mushrooms in boiling water for about 20 minutes, until they are completely reconstituted.

Step 4 Remove the hard stalks from the Chinese mushrooms and discard them. Slice the caps finely.

1. Soak the mushrooms in enough hot water to cover for 20 minutes, or until completely reconstituted.

2. Heat the vegetable oil in a wok or frying pan, and add the prawns, chillies, lemon rind and spring onions. Stir-fry quickly for 1 minute.

3. Add the stock, the Worcestershire sauce and the soy sauce. Bring this mixture to the boil, reduce the heat and simmer for 5 minutes. Season to taste.

4. Remove the stalks from the mushrooms and discard them. Slice the caps very finely.

5. Cut the fish into small pieces, and add to the soup, together with the bean curd and Chinese mushrooms. Simmer for 5 minutes.

6. Stir in the lemon juice and sesame seeds. Adjust the seasoning and serve sprinkled with chopped fresh coriander leaves, if desired.

Chilli Vegetable Soup

SERVES 4

This simple-to-make soup makes a light first course.

PREPARATION: 40 mins
COOKING: 20 mins

Taco Sauce
1 tbsp oil
1 onion, diced
1 green pepper, diced
½-1 red or green chilli pepper, chopped
½ tsp ground cumin
½ tsp ground coriander
½ clove garlic, crushed
Pinch salt, pepper and sugar
400g/14oz tinned tomatoes
Tomato purée

1 tbsp oil
1 onion, chopped
120g/4oz tinned whole green chillies,
    quartered
1 litre/2 pints chicken stock
1 large potato, peeled and cut into short strips
1 tbsp lime juice
Tortilla chips and lime slices to garnish

1. Heat the oil in a heavy-based saucepan, add the onion and pepper and cook slowly to soften slightly.

Step 5 Add the remaining ingredients and simmer for 20 minutes.

2. Add the chilli, cumin, coriander and garlic and cook a further 2-3 minutes.

3. Add sugar, seasonings and tomatoes with their juice. Break up the tomatoes with a fork or a potato masher.

4. Cook a further 5-6 minutes over moderate heat to reduce. Add tomato purée for colour, if necessary. Season to taste.

5. Heat the remaining oil in a large saucepan and sauté the onion until translucent. Add the chillies, stock, potato and pre-prepared taco sauce.

6. Cover the pan and simmer soup for 20 minutes. Stir in the lime juice and add salt.

7. Serve in individual bowls with tortilla chips. Cut a thin slice of lime to float in each bowl of soup.

Samosas

SERVES 6

These Indian snacks can be eaten either hot or cold.

PREPARATION: 40 mins
COOKING: 25 mins

Pastry
275g/10oz plain flour
¼ tsp salt
¼ tsp baking powder
Water, to mix

Filling
3 tbsps oil
1 medium onion, chopped
450g/1lb potatoes, cut into small dice
2 carrots, grated
60g/2oz green peas, shelled
60g/2oz green beans, chopped
1 tsp chilli powder
1 tsp salt
1 tsp garam masala
½ tsp ground turmeric
1 tbsp lemon juice
Oil for deep frying

1. Make the pastry by sifting the flour, salt and baking powder into a bowl and adding enough water, a little at a time, to mix to a soft dough. Cover and leave to stand for 30 minutes.

2. Heat the 3 tbsps oil and fry the onion until it is just soft. Stir in the potatoes and carrots and cook for 3-4 minutes.

Step 6 Fill each cone with a little of the vegetable mixture.

3. Add the peas and beans to the potato mixture, cook for a further 2 minutes, then stir in the spices and lemon juice. Cover and simmer until the potatoes are tender. Remove from the heat and allow to cool.

4. Divide the dough into 12 equal-sized balls. Roll each piece out on a floured board, to a thin circle about 15cm/6 inches in diameter.

5. Cut each circle in half. Dampen the straight edges of each semicircle and bring them together, overlapping slightly to make a cone.

6. Fill each cone with a little of the filling, then dampen the open edge and seal by pressing together firmly. For extra firmness dampen and fold this edge over.

7. Heat the oil for frying. Fry the samosas, a few at a time, until they are golden brown. Drain on absorbent kitchen paper.

Lamb Korma

SERVES 4

Lamb Korma, a rich, spicy dish, is one of the best known of the Indian curries.

PREPARATION: 15 mins
COOKING: 40-50 mins

Step 1 Fry the whole spices with the onion for 1 minute.

3 tbsps vegetable oil
1 medium onion, sliced
2.5cm/1-inch piece cinnamon stick
6 cloves
Seeds of 6 small cardamoms
1 bay leaf
1 tsp black cumin seeds
2 tsps grated ginger
2 cloves garlic, crushed
450g/1lb shoulder of lamb, cubed
1 tsp chilli powder
1 tsp ground coriander
2 tsps ground cumin
¼ tsp ground turmeric
140ml/¼ pint natural yogurt
160ml/6 fl oz water
1 tbsp ground almonds
2 green chillies, halved and seeded
2 sprigs fresh coriander leaves, chopped

1. Fry the onion in the oil until golden brown. Add the cinnamon, cloves, cardamom seeds, bay leaf and the cumin seeds. Fry for 1 minute.

2. Add the ginger and garlic and the cubed lamb. Sprinkle over the chilli powder, ground coriander, cumin and turmeric and mix together well.

3. Stir in the yogurt, cover the pan and cook over a moderate heat for 10-15 minutes, stirring occasionally.

4. Add the water and season, re-cover and simmer gently for 30-40 minutes, or until the meat is tender.

5. Just before serving, add the almonds, chillies and coriander leaves. Stir in a little more water if necessary.

Step 3 Stir the yogurt into the lamb korma, and mix well, to blend thoroughly.

Curried Pork Stew

SERVES 4

This savoury stew requires long, slow cooking to bring out its flavour.

PREPARATION: 25 mins
COOKING: 1 hr 30 mins

900g/2lb pork shoulder, cut in 5cm/2 inch
   cubes
2 tbsps oil
2 medium onions, coarsely chopped
1 large green pepper, seeded and coarsely
   chopped
1 tbsp curry powder
2 cloves garlic, crushed
450g/1lb tinned tomatoes
3 tbsps tomato purée
140ml/¼ pint water or beef stock
2 tbsps cider vinegar
1 bay leaf
½ tsp dried mint
A few drops tabasco sauce

Step 4 When the meat is tender, skim excess fat from the surface of the sauce with a spoon.

Step 2 Combine the ingredients and stir well to break up the tomatoes slightly.

1. Heat about 2 tbsps oil in a large frying pan. When hot, add the pork cubes in two batches. Brown over high heat for about 5 minutes per batch, then reserve. Add more oil if necessary and cook the onions and peppers to soften. Add the curry powder and garlic and cook 1 minute more.

2. Add the tomatoes, their juice and the tomato purée. Stir in the water or stock and vinegar breaking up the tomatoes slightly. Add bay leaf, mint and then season.

3. Transfer to a casserole dish. Bring the mixture to the boil and then cook slowly for about 1½ hours, covered.

4. When the meat is tender, skim any fat from the surface of the sauce, remove the bay leaf and add a few drops of tabasco sauce to taste.

Spare Ribs in Chilli and Cream Sauce

SERVES 4

Unsweetened cocoa lends colour and depth to a sauce for ribs.

PREPARATION: 20 mins
COOKING: 50-55 mins

1kg/2¼lbs spare ribs
1 tsp cocoa powder
1 tbsp flour
½ tsp cumin
½ tsp paprika
½ tsp dried oregano, crushed
280ml/½ pint warm water
2 tbsps thin honey
2 tbsps double cream
Lime wedges and watercress for garnish

---

1. Leave the ribs in whole slabs and roast at

Step 1 Cook the ribs until well browned. Remove from the roasting pan and pour off the fat.

Step 3 Place ribs on a chopping board and cut into pieces.

200°C/400°F/Gas Mark 6 for 20-25 minutes, or until well browned. Drain off all the excess fat.

2. Blend together the cocoa, flour, cumin, paprika, oregano, water and honey, and season well. Pour over the ribs. Lower the temperature to 180°C/350°F/Gas Mark 4 and cook ribs for a further 30 minutes, until the sauce has reduced and the ribs are tender.

3. Cut the ribs into pieces and arrange on a serving dish.

4. Pour the cream into the sauce in the roasting pan and place over moderate heat. Bring to the boil and pour over the ribs.

5. Garnish with lime wedges and serve.

Albóndigas
(Meatballs)

SERVES 4

These hot, spicy meatballs make a tasty supper dish.

PREPARATION: 25 mins
COOKING: 20 mins

225g/8oz minced veal
225g/8oz minced beef
1 clove garlic, crushed
2 tbsps dry breadcrumbs
½ chilli pepper, seeded and finely chopped
½ tsp ground cumin
1 egg, beaten
3 tbsps oil
280ml/½ pint Taco Sauce (see Chilli Vegetable Soup)
2 spring onions, chopped

---

1. Mix together the veal, beef, garlic, breadcrumbs, chilli pepper, cumin and season well. Add the egg gradually until well-blended.

Step 3 Flour hands well and roll each piece into a ball.

Step 5 Brown the meatballs on all sides in hot oil until a good colour.

2. Turn the mixture out onto a floured surface and divide into 16 equal pieces.

3. With floured hands, shape the mixture into balls.

4. Pour about 3 tbsps of oil into a large frying pan and place over high heat.

5. When the oil is hot, place in the meatballs and fry for 5-10 minutes until brown on all sides. Turn frequently during cooking.

6. Remove the browned meatballs and drain well on paper towels. Place in an ovenproof dish and pour over the taco sauce.

7. Heat through in a preheated 170°C/350°F/ Gas Mark 3 oven for 10 minutes. Sprinkle with chopped onions to serve.

Chilli Beef Stew

SERVES 6-8

Red onions, red peppers, tomatoes and red beans all go into this zesty stew.

PREPARATION: 25 mins
COOKING: 1-2 hrs

900g/2lbs chuck steak, cut into 2.5cm/1 inch
  pieces
4 tbsps oil
1 large red onion, coarsely chopped
2 cloves garlic, crushed
2 red peppers, seeded and roughly chopped
1-2 red chillies, seeded and finely chopped
3 tbsps mild chilli powder
1 tbsp cumin
1 tbsp paprika
700ml/1½ pints beer, water or stock
225g/8oz tinned tomatoes, puréed
2 tbsps tomato purée
225g/8oz tinned red kidney beans, drained
Pinch salt
6 ripe tomatoes, peeled, seeded and diced

Step 2 Cook the onions, garlic, red peppers and chillies slowly until slightly softened.

Step 2 If using beer, add it very slowly as it will tend to foam up in the heat of the pan.

1. Pour the oil into a flameproof casserole. When hot, brown the meat in small batches over moderately high heat for about 5 minutes per batch.

2. Set aside the meat on a plate. Lower the heat and cook the onion, garlic, red peppers and chillies for about 5 minutes. Add the chilli powder, cumin and paprika and cook for 1 minute further. Pour on the liquid and add the tinned tomatoes, tomato purée and the meat.

3. Cook slowly for about 1½-2 hours. Add the beans about 45 minutes before the end of cooking time.

4. When the meat is tender, add salt to taste and serve garnished with diced tomatoes.

Tamarind Chicken Satay

SERVES 4

Tomato and chilli sambal makes the perfect accompaniment for this dish.

PREPARATION: 30 mins
COOKING: 10-15 mins

---

4 chicken breasts, skinned, boned and cut into
   1.25cm/½ inch cubes

Marinade
1 tbsp oil
5cm/2 inch piece tamarind, soaked in 100ml/
   4 fl oz hot water or lemon juice
2 cloves garlic, crushed
1 tsp ground cardamom
½ tsp ground nutmeg
Salt and pepper
1 tsp sweet soy sauce

Tomato and Chilli Sambal
2 red chilli peppers
1 small piece fresh ginger, grated
1 clove garlic, crushed
450g/1lb fresh tomatoes, peeled and seeded
4 tbsps oil
1 tbsp lemon or lime juice
1 tbsp dark brown sugar
Salt and pepper

---

1. Put the chicken in a large bowl. Mix together the marinade ingredients and pour them over the chicken. Stir well and refrigerate for at least 30 minutes.

Step 6 Cook the chicken skewers under a preheated grill. Baste them with the remaining marinade as they cook.

2. Grind together the chillies, ginger and garlic. Chop the tomatoes coarsely and blend them into the chilli mixture.

3. Heat the oil in a wok or large frying pan and fry the tomato mixture for about 5-6 minutes, stirring occasionally to prevent it sticking. Add the lemon juice and a spoonful of water, if the sauce becomes too thick.

4. Stir in the sugar and seasoning to taste.

5. Thread the marinated chicken cubes onto thin wooden skewers.

6. Cook the chicken under a preheated grill, turning frequently, until golden brown, about 5-8 minutes. Brush the chicken with the remaining marinade during cooking.

Plaice with Spicy Tomato Sauce

SERVES 4

This piquant fish dish is popular along Mexico's Gulf coast.

PREPARATION: 30 mins
COOKING: 20-25 mins

90g/3oz cream cheese
1 tsp dried oregano
Pinch cayenne pepper
4 whole fillets of plaice
Lime slices and dill to garnish

Tomato Sauce
1 tbsp oil
1 small onion, chopped
1 stick celery, chopped
1 chilli pepper, seeded and chopped
¼ tsp each ground cumin, coriander and ginger
½ red and ½ green pepper, seeded and
    chopped
400g/14oz tinned tomatoes
1 tbsp tomato purée
Salt, pepper and a pinch sugar

1. Heat the oil in a heavy-based pan and cook the onion, celery, chilli pepper and spices for about 5 minutes over very low heat.

2. Add the remaining ingredients and bring to the boil. Reduce heat and simmer 15-20 minutes, stirring occasionally. Set aside.

Step 6 Spread cheese filling on the fish and roll up each fillet.

3. Mix the cream cheese, oregano and cayenne pepper together and set aside.

4. Skin the fillets, starting at the tail end and hold the knife at a slight angle to the skin.

5. Push the knife along using a sawing motion, with the blade against the skin. Dip fingers in salt to make it easier to hold onto the fish skin. Gradually separate the fish from the skin.

6. Spread the cheese filling on all 4 fillets and roll each up. Secure with cocktail sticks.

7. Place the fillets in a lightly greased baking dish, cover and cook for 10 minutes in a preheated 180°C/350°F/Gas Mark 4 oven.

8. Pour over the tomato sauce and cook a further 10-15 minutes. Fish is cooked when it feels firm and looks opaque. Garnish with lime slices and dill.

Coconut Fried Fish with Chillies

SERVES 4

A real treat for lovers of spicy food.

PREPARATION: 30 mins
COOKING: 30 mins

Oil for frying
450g/1lb sole or plaice fillets, skinned, boned
    and cut into 2.5cm/1-inch strips
Seasoned flour
1 egg, beaten
60g/2oz desiccated coconut
1 tbsp vegetable oil
1 tsp grated fresh ginger
¼ tsp chilli powder
1 red chilli, seeded and finely chopped
1 tsp ground coriander
½ tsp ground nutmeg
1 clove garlic, crushed
2 tbsps tomato purée
2 tbsps tomato chutney
2 tbsps dark soy sauce
2 tbsps lemon juice
2 tbsps water
1 tsp brown sugar
Salt and pepper

1. In a frying pan, heat about 5cm/2 inches of oil to 190°C/375°F. Toss the fish strips in the seasoned flour and then dip them into the beaten egg. Roll them in the desiccated coconut and shake off the excess.

Step 1 Toss the strips of fish in the flour and then dip them in the beaten egg. Roll them finally in the desiccated coconut.

2. Fry the fish, a few pieces at a time, in the hot oil and drain them on absorbent kitchen paper. Keep warm.

3. Heat the 1 tbsp oil in a wok or frying pan and fry the ginger, red chilli, spices and garlic, for about 2 minutes.

4. Add the remaining ingredients and simmer for about 3 minutes. Serve the fish, with the sauce handed round separately.

Step 2 Fry the fish in the hot oil, a few pieces at a time, to prevent it from breaking up.

Cod Curry

SERVES 4

The fragrant spices used in this recipe complement the fish perfectly.

PREPARATION: 15 mins
COOKING: 20 mins

3 tbsps vegetable oil
1 large onion, finely chopped
2.5cm/1-inch piece cinnamon stick
1 bay leaf
1 tsp ginger paste
1 tsp garlic paste
1 tsp chilli powder
1 tsp ground cumin
1 tsp ground coriander
¼ tsp ground turmeric
140ml/¼ pint natural yogurt OR
225g/8oz tinned tomatoes, chopped
1-2 fresh green chillies, chopped
2 sprigs fresh coriander leaves, chopped
1 tsp salt
450g/1lb cod cutlets, or fillets, cut into 5cm/
    2-inch pieces

1. In a large heavy-based saucepan, fry the onion in the oil until golden brown. Add the cinnamon, bay leaf, ginger and garlic pastes and fry for 1 minute.

2. Add the ground spices and fry for a further minute, then stir in *either* the yogurt, *or* the tinned tomatoes and the chopped chillies and coriander leaves.

Step 1 Fry the cinnamon, bay leaf and the ginger and garlic pastes with the onions for 1 minute.

3. Only if you have used yogurt, stir in 140ml/¼ pint water and simmer the mixture for 2-3 minutes. Do not add any water if you have used the tinned tomatoes.

4. Stir the cod into the sauce, and add the salt. Cover the pan and simmer for 15-18 minutes before serving.

Step 4 Add the cod pieces to the sauce in the pan, stir well to coat thoroughly, before covering and simmering for 15-18 minutes.

Chilli Prawn Quiche

SERVES 6

Fresh chilli peppers give a Mexican flavour to this quiche.

PREPARATION: 40 mins, including time for the pastry to chill
COOKING: 30-40 mins

Pastry
120g/4oz plain flour
Pinch salt
2 tbsps butter or margarine
2 tbsps white cooking fat
2-4 tbsps cold water

Filling
4 eggs
140ml/¼ pint milk
140ml/¼ pint single cream
½ clove garlic, crushed
120g/4oz Cheddar cheese, grated
3 spring onions, chopped
2 green chillies, seeded and chopped
225g/8oz cooked and peeled prawns
Cooked, unpeeled prawns and parsley sprigs
for garnish

1. Sift the flour with a pinch of salt into a mixing bowl.

2. Rub in the butter and fat until the mixture resembles fine breadcrumbs.

3. Mix in the liquid gradually, adding enough to bring the pastry together into a ball.

4. Wrap the pastry well and chill for 30 minutes.

Step 6 Use the rolling pin to help lift the pastry into the flan dish.

5. Roll out the pastry on a well-floured surface with a floured rolling pin.

6. Wrap the pastry around the rolling pin to lift it into a 25cm/10 inch flan dish.

7. Carefully press the pastry onto the bottom and up the sides of the dish.

8. Roll the rolling pin over the top of the dish to remove excess pastry.

9. Mix the eggs, milk, cream and garlic together and lightly season. Sprinkle the cheese, spring onion, chillies and prawns onto the base of the pastry and pour over the egg mixture.

10. Bake in a preheated 200°C/400°F/Gas Mark 6 oven for 30-40 minutes until firm and golden brown. Peel the tail shells off the prawns and remove the legs and roe if present. Use to garnish the quiche along with the sprigs of parsley.

Egg Curry

SERVES 4

Quick and easy, this curry is a delicious way of serving hard-boiled eggs.

PREPARATION: 10 mins
COOKING: 20 mins

4-6 eggs
1 large onion, finely chopped
1 tbsp oil
2.5cm/1 inch stick cinnamon
1 bay leaf
4 small cardamoms
6 cloves
1 tsp garlic paste
1 tsp ginger paste
1 tsp ground coriander
1 tsp ground cumin
¼ tsp ground turmeric
1 tsp garam masala
1 tsp chilli powder
225g/8oz tinned tomatoes, crushed
Salt to taste
180ml/6 fl oz water or vegetable stock
2 sprigs fresh coriander leaves
2 green chillies

---

1. Hard-boil the eggs for 8-10 minutes. Cool them completely in cold water, then remove the shells.

2. Heat the oil in a large saucepan and fry the onion gently until it is soft, but not browned.

Step 5 Put the hard-boiled eggs into the curry sauce, stir well and cook for 10-12 minutes.

3. Add the cinnamon, bay leaf, cardamoms and cloves and fry for 1 minute. Stir in the ginger and garlic pastes. Add the coriander, cumin, turmeric, garam masala and chilli powder. Stir together well and fry for 30 seconds.

4. Add the tomatoes and salt to the spices. Stir in well and simmer for 5 minutes. Add the water or stock, and bring the mixture to the boil.

5. Put the eggs into the curry sauce and simmer for 10-12 minutes.

6. Chop the coriander leaves and the green chillies finely, and sprinkle them over the cooked eggs, to garnish.

Penne with Spicy Chilli Sauce

SERVES 4-6

Penne are hollow pasta tubes which can be bought at most supermarkets.

PREPARATION: 15 mins
COOKING: 30 mins

450g/1lb tinned tomatoes
1 tbsp olive oil
2 cloves garlic, crushed
1 onion, chopped
4 rashers of bacon, chopped
2 red chilli peppers, seeded and chopped
2 spring onions, chopped
60g/2oz Parmesan cheese, grated
450g/1lb penne or macaroni
Salt and pepper

Step 3 Stir the sieved tomatoes, chilli peppers, spring onions and half the cheese into the onion mixture.

Step 5 Toss the cooked penne in half of the sauce, mixing together well to coat evenly.

1. Chop the tomatoes and sieve them to remove the pips.

2. Heat the oil in a frying pan and fry the garlic, onion and bacon gently for 6-8 minutes.

3. Add the sieved tomatoes, the chilli peppers, spring onions and half of the cheese. Simmer gently for 20 minutes.

4. Cook the penne or macaroni in boiling water for 10-15 minutes. Rinse under hot water and drain well.

5. Put the cooked penne into a warm serving dish and toss them in half of the sauce. Pour the remaining sauce over the top and sprinkle with the remaining cheese.

Spicy Rice and Bean Pilaff

SERVES 6-8

This recipe can either be served as a side dish or vegetarian main course.

PREPARATION: 25 mins
COOKING: 50 mins

4 tbsps oil
225g/8oz long grain rice
1 onion, finely chopped
1 green pepper, seeded and chopped
1 tsp each each ground cumin and coriander
Dash tabasco sauce
Salt
1 litre/1¾ pints vegetable stock
450g/1lb canned red kidney beans, drained
450g/1lb canned tomatoes, drained and
  coarsely chopped
Chopped parsley

Step 2 Cook the rice in the oil until just turning opaque.

Step 3 Cook with the remaining ingredients until rice is tender and most of the liquid is absorbed.

1. Heat the oil in a casserole or large saucepan.

2. Add the rice and cook until just turning opaque. Add the onion, pepper and cumin and coriander. Cook gently for a further 2 minutes.

3. Add the tabasco, salt, stock and beans and bring to the boil. Cover and cook about 45 minutes, or until the rice is tender and most of the liquid is absorbed.

4. Remove from the heat and add the tomatoes, stirring them in gently. Leave to stand, covered, for 5 minutes.

5. Fluff up the mixture with a fork and sprinkle with parsley to serve.

Oriental Noodles

SERVES 4

A most versatile vegetable dish, this goes well with meat or can stand alone.

PREPARATION: 25 mins
COOKING: 7-8 mins

225g/8oz Chinese noodles (medium thickness)
5 tbsps oil
4 carrots, peeled
225g/8oz broccoli
12 Chinese mushrooms, soaked 30 minutes
1 clove garlic, peeled
4 spring onions, diagonally sliced
1-2 tbsps chilli sauce, mild or hot
4 tbsps soy sauce
4 tbsps rice wine or dry sherry
2 tsps cornflour

Step 7 Cook vegetables and sauce ingredients until cornflour thickens and clears.

1. Cook noodles in boiling salted water for about 4-5 minutes. Drain well, rinse under hot water and drain again. Toss with 1 tbsp of the oil to prevent sticking.

2. Slice the carrots thinly on the diagonal.

3. Cut the florets off the stems of the brocolli and divide into even-sized but not too small sections. Slice the stalks thinly on the diagonal.

4. Place the vegetables in boiling water for about 2 minutes to blanch. Drain and rinse under cold water and leave to drain.

5. Remove and discard the mushroom stems and slice the caps thinly.

6. Heat a wok and add the remaining oil with the garlic clove. Leave the garlic in the pan while the oil heats and then remove it. Add the carrots and broccoli and stir-fry about 1 minute. Add mushrooms and onions and continue to stir-fry, tossing the vegetables in the pan continuously.

7. Combine chilli sauce, soy sauce, wine and cornflour. Pour over the vegetables and cook until the sauce clears. Toss with the noodles and heat them through and serve immediately.

Aubergines and Peppers Szechuan Style

SERVES 4

Authentic Szechuan food is fiery hot. Outside China, restaurants often tone down the taste for Western palates.

PREPARATION: 30 mins
COOKING: 7-8 mins

1 large aubergine
2 cloves garlic, crushed
2.5cm/1-inch piece fresh ginger, finely
  chopped
1 onion, roughly chopped
1 small green pepper, roughly chopped
1 small red pepper, roughly chopped
1 red or green chilli, seeded, cored and cut into
  thin strips
120ml/4 fl oz chicken or vegetable stock
1 tsp sugar
1 tsp vinegar
Salt and pepper
1 tsp cornflour
1 tbsp soy sauce
Sesame oil
6 tbsps oil

Step 1 Cut the aubergine in half and lightly score the surface.

1. Cut the aubergines in half and score the surface.

2. Sprinkle lightly with salt and leave to drain in a colander or on paper towels for 30 minutes.

3. After 30 minutes, squeeze the aubergine gently to extract any bitter juices and rinse thoroughly under cold water. Pat dry and cut the aubergine into 2.5cm/1 inch cubes.

4. Heat about 3 tbsps oil in a wok. Add the aubergine and stir-fry for about 4-5 minutes. It may be necessary to add more oil as the aubergine cooks. Remove from the wok and set aside.

5. Reheat the wok and add 2 tbsps oil. Add the garlic and ginger and stir-fry for 1 minute. Add the onions and stir-fry for 2 minutes. Add the green pepper, red pepper and chilli pepper and stir-fry for 1 minute. Return the aubergine to the wok along with the remaining ingredients.

6. Bring to the boil, stirring constantly, and cook until the sauce thickens and clears. Serve immediately.

Index

Chilli Beef Stew makes a delicious supper dish.